CAPTURE
YOUR AUDIENCE
THROUGH
STORYTELLING

A guide for
speakers and executives

THELMA L. WELLS

Illustrated by
Mike Placier

KENDALL/HUNT PUBLISHING COMPANY
4050 Westmark Drive   Dubuque, Iowa 52002

CAPTURE YOUR AUDIENCE THROUGH STORYTELLING
A guide for speakers and executives

Copyright © 1994 by Thelma Wells and Associates

ISBN 0-7872-0095-6

Library of Congress Catalog Card No. 94-79025

Printed in the United States of America

10 9 8 7 6 5 4 3 2 1

To my family . . .
for your love, understanding and support. Thank you.

In Christ, you can BE
the best of who you
want to
BEE !

Acknowledgements

When I married my husband, George Wells, 32 years ago, I never dreamed that he would push me, support me, console me, adore me, trust me and love me as he does. But in every venture I take, he's right there all the way. Thank you, Honey, for being flesh of my flesh and bone of my bone.

Proverbs 31 says that "her children shall rise up and call her blessed." The greatest compliment a mother can receive is from the support and praise of her children. Vikki, George F., and Lesa express their love and respect for me in all I do. They sing my praises. I bless them as they bless me.

Special thanks to Antony, my grandson, who makes me happy by "doing the right thing"; to my mother, Dorothy Calhoun who through sickness and paralysis continues to watch, fight and pray for me; to my sister, Sarah Stinnett, for praying for me and encouraging me. Daddy William Harrell, Granny Sarah Harrell and Daddy Lawrence Morris are all responsible for my positive attitude, determination, moral character and Christian upbringing. May they rest in peace with Jesus.

To those who helped get this project finished, thank you—
    Vikki Wells for her creative writing skills.
    Ed Newsome for his journalistic expertise.
    Dave Gorden and Nido Qubein for their professional opinions.
    Suzanne Boswell, Sharon Egiebor and Michael Mullins for their expert editorial assistance.
    Mary Bold and Evan Fogelman for their publishing insights.
    Beverly Walls, Gwendolyn Brown and Elizabeth Love for their proofreading assistance.
    Reggie Johnson for his production assistance.

God bless you all . . .

Foreword

You have made an investment, when you obtained this book, that will definitely pay off in great dividends for you. As you read, you will be enlightened, inspired, entertained, educated and enriched.

Whether you speak to groups on a regular basis, lead a meeting occasionally, teach a class, manage a sales force or make a presentation from time to time, the application of this material will make you more effective. Storytelling is an art and a tradition that has survived through the ages, because it is a powerful and effective way to help people understand a point.

Thelma Wells has truly mastered the art of "Storytelling." She walks her talk; she knows how to draw word pictures that you can see with your mind's eye. I am proud to be a colleague of Thelma's through our affiliation with the National Speakers Association. After seeing her work with an audience that was standing room only (as a matter of fact, folks were lined up in the hall), I am sure you will be enriched from having read this book.

The checklist at the back of the book will help you apply the principles that are contained in a practical, step by step manner. Remember, practice brings improvement, so review the ideas contained and apply them as often as possible.

In the opinion of many, Thelma Wells is a storyteller's storyteller; turn the page, start reading and you will begin to see why.

Dave Gorden

Contents

PART 1
Deciding To Tell A Story

PART 2
Researching The Story

PART 3
Telling The Story

Stories can . . .

encourage, inspire, instruct, illustrate, illuminate, motivate, enhance, enrich and entertain.

Introduction

Preparing to make a speech is like assembling a jigsaw puzzle; there are many pieces. This book is a resource written to guide you through one piece of the speech—storytelling.

Storytelling is an art. Regardless of whether it's a keynote address or training session, it is an invaluable addition to a successful speech. People love stories. They seem to have the power to move people to action. Many people learn faster if they hear a story. The story becomes real to them as they visualize its action. The ability to mentally visualize the action helps people connect to the concept and idea. The subject matter then comes to life.

Storytelling has been used for centuries as a way to pass on news, facts, data and knowledge. Civilizations, cultures, communities and families have used storytelling as a means to document information throughout history. Storytelling is as old as the first human beings.

The First Story

Come with me to the Garden of Eden. See the colorful foliage in beautiful hues of red, yellow, blue and green. Feel the spring breeze. Let's play with the animals and visit with Adam and Eve.

As the story goes, Adam is busy naming everything. On this particular day, Eve is a little bored; so she spends her afternoon talking about life with her pet serpent. They talk about how terrific God is and how it would be cool to be like Him.

She wonders, "If I eat from that tree over there, will I really be like God?" She decides to check it out. She goes over to the tree. You know, the one in the middle of the garden. She looks at it. It looks delicious. She decides to take just one little bite and give the rest to Adam. She eats. Adam eats. God gets mad. (thunder/lightning). "Adam! Adam! I told you not to eat of THAT tree!" God shouts. Adam, feeling a little nervous, thinks fast and replies, "Wait God, let me tell you a story. You see . . ."

This is my interpretation of the story of Adam and Eve, but you get the point—stories have been around a long, long time. On the surface, stories seem easy to tell. But have you ever heard a story that seemed to go on and on forever? Have you ever listened to a story and wondered "what's the point?" Have you ever heard a story that was just down right vulgar?

As speakers, trainers and managers, our stories must teach, move to action and guide our listeners to new heights. Certainly, the best speakers and trainers are also the best storytellers.

Why should you use storytelling in your presentations?

    * *It's simple.* Everyone has stories. People love to hear them and love to tell them. Stories can make your point much easier to understand.

    * *It's effective.* Stories can help bring the listener to a desired result and enable the listener to retain your message long after the presentation is over.

    * *It's timeless.* Stories transcend time. Incidents that happened decades ago can be just as timely now when presented in story form.

    * *It's unifying.* Stories tend to unite the audience to a common goal or mission regardless of race, religion, geographic location, educational background, gender or age.

This book will help you become a more effective storyteller. It is in question and answer form to make it easy for you to follow. Throughout you will find strategies, methods, techniques and examples of stories that will steer you on your way to *capturing your audience through storytelling.*

PART 1

Deciding To Tell A Story

Stories can . . .

set the stage for a great speech.

QUESTION 1

What Point Do I Want To Make?

Putting together pieces of a puzzle can mean many hours of fun. With little practice, anyone can learn simple techniques to use. Preparing a speech is much like putting together the pieces of a jigsaw puzzle. One of the most important pieces is "storytelling."

When deciding to tell a story, you want to insure that the story either entertains, fascinates, informs or mystifies the audience. The story should hit the mind of the reader and make a specific point. The story should always supplement the point of emphasis, be time-sensitive and create a sense of appreciation.

For example, one of the first statements I make when introducing myself to an audience is, "Please call me Thelma—not Mrs. Wells." So I tell a story.

My Mother-in-law

Mrs. Wells is my mother-in-law. I never say that when she's with me because she gets angry. I took her to Lawton, Okla., and I asked the audience to call me Thelma. "Please don't call me Mrs. Wells," I said, "because Mrs. Wells is my mother-in-law." When we got into the car, she reprimanded me. She said, "Why did you say that?" I said, "It gets a laugh." "It's not funny," she said. So I promised her I would never do that again (when she's with me).

15

I tell this story often when I am introducing myself because I want to make several points. First, I want the audience to remember my name. Second, I want to give them permission to use my first name and I ask them if I may call them by their first names. Third, I want to relax the listener. This story breaks the formality and makes the audience laugh. Consequently, a story at the start of a speech can set the atmosphere for the rest of the presentation.

When deciding to tell a story, ask yourself if you are telling a story just for the sake of telling a story, or telling it to illustrate a particular point.

"Make A Point—Tell A Story"

Maybe you have heard great speakers say "make a point—tell a story." This advice is like eating your favorite food—it's good. By making a point first, then telling your story, you clarify your point in the mind of the listener. Let me give you an example.

The Piano Player

I teach people to "eliminate the negatives" from their lives. Everyone has talents, skills and abilities that are unique to each of us. If we specialize in our God-given talents and solicit help for the things we just can't seem to master, we can begin to eliminate some of those negative feelings from our lives.

I have a friend named Dr. Shirley Harris. She plays the piano beautifully. I wanted to learn to play the piano like Dr. Shirley Harris. She can listen to anything—Bach, Beethoven, Gospel, Rock 'N Roll—and sit down and play it by ear. I thought, "I can sing, so I bet I can also play the piano. I'll pay for piano lessons!" For four-and-a-half years, I sat at my piano taking lessons. Four-and-a-half years, noise came out of the piano. I even had it tuned, noise! I envied Shirley. I coveted her talent.

16

One day in disgust, I was sitting at my piano and thought, "Why can't I play like Shirley? Shirley thinks she can sing, but she can't. I know I can sing, but I can't play." Then the light in my mind came on. "Why not call Shirley and ask her to play for me when I sing." I picked up the phone, called Shirley, and asked, "Shirley, would you like to play for me when I go to sing?" She said, "Thelma Wells, I was wondering when you were going to ask me." Now, when we go out to perform, we are a dynamic duo. So don't let your shortcomings get you down; delegate to someone—hire it out or barter it done. But, eliminate negative feelings from your life.

Notice I first emphasized a point—you can "eliminate the negatives" from your life. Then I chose to illustrate this point with a story. I selected this particular story because it gives an example of negative feelings I had toward a good friend. It shows how my feelings changed when I began to focus on my positive talents and utilize the talents of another to enhance my overall position. I made a point, then told a story.

A practical story can help listeners reflect on their situations and prompt them to take positive action. When you make a point and tell a story, make sure your story makes your point come to life for the listener. I could have thought of other stories to use to create emphasis. In fact, it may have been more appropriate for me to use another story with a different audience. Regardless of the anecdote you choose, each story should mirror your point. Many times the story will be remembered long after the point is forgotten. Remembering the story will trigger the listener to recall the point.

QUESTION 2

Do I Know How To Tell The Story And Make It Powerful?

Learning to tell a story with impact takes practice. As you practice, you'll want to record yourself, observe yourself in a mirror and have good honest friends listen to your speech. You'll need:

Tape recorder. Record your practice sessions and listen to them. This takes guts because most of us hate the way we sound on tape. Nonetheless, as you listen to your stories on tape, you'll learn a lot about your content and overall presentation. You'll be able to hear your enthusiasm or lack thereof. You'll notice unclear points. You'll easily pick up distracting words like "well", "ah" and "you see." Listening to yourself might take getting used to, but it's worth it. Get attached to your recorder and start taking it everywhere you go. Not only will listening to yourself enhance your stories, but if you keep your recorder with you, you'll be able to tape new stories while they are fresh on your mind.

Mirror. Stand in front of a mirror and practice your stories. This might seem silly, even embarrassing, but it's amazing what you will find you do with your hands, feet, lips, eyes and head as you speak. Most of us have some irritating habit we do while we are talking. As you view yourself while practicing, you'll learn to break any annoying habits. I used to suck my teeth. Yuk!

18

True friends. I say true friends because it can be embarrassing to have someone tell you you're awful or your story makes no sense. But a true friend can be honest without destroying your self-esteem. In fact, it's better that you get an honest opinion than a sugar-coated one for fear of hurting your feelings.

Ask your friends: Do you know the point of my story? Can you identify with the message? Does my story flow? Is it too long or short? Do I have enough emphasis, pauses, tone inflections? Do I appear sincere? Was I making any awkward motions or sounds? True friends will offer candid suggestions to improve your stories.

Proper Preparation Produces Powerful Parables

QUESTION 3

Do I Have Adequate Time For A Story?

I was speaking at a showcase for the North Texas Speakers Association several years ago. Just a few seconds before I was scheduled to speak, the program director whispered, "Cut it short, to about three minutes; we're out of time." Can you imagine? I had practiced my speech complete with stories and I thought it was good just the way I had rehearsed it. In a moment's notice, I had to create a short version to my stories. This incident taught me two valuable lessons: Be prepared and flexible when practicing the material.

Practice telling stories several different ways
without omitting vital information.

Mrs. Thompson
(long version)

Are any of you related to Mrs. Thompson in Dallas? I hope not. I met Mrs. Thompson when I was in charge of the customer service area at NorthPark National Bank a number of years ago. As the customer service manager, I would always tell my staff to come and get me if they encountered customers they couldn't handle. I had also taught them never to tell customers that a bank representative could not help them; rather, tell them what could be done to assist them.

Early one Monday morning a clerk came and got me. Mrs. Thompson was there. They had tried to tell Mrs. Thompson everything that they could do for her, but she didn't like that. So I went to speak to Mrs. Thompson. Mrs. Thompson "cussed" me. (There's a difference between cursing and cussing.) Mrs. Thompson "cussed" me! She called me fat, black, ugly and short. She

21

resurrected my ancestors and then put them back in the grave. She even talked about my mama. I stood there quite controlled. Everyone, including those who usually were on a coffee break, stood there and stared in disbelief. Finally when she finished, I told her again what we could do for her. This time, she added animation to her verbal abuse. She used fingers and other body parts. When she finally decided to leave, a man came over to me and said, "Madam, how could you stand there and take that from that woman? I would have pulled her over the counter." I replied, "Sir, I wasn't going down to her level. I was doing everything I could to help her and I'm none of those things she called me."

Six years later, Mrs. Thompson attended a seminar I was conducting. She came up to me and asked a silly question. She asked, "Do you remember me?" I replied, "I do." As she talked, I realized that she had come to the seminar especially to see me. For six years, she had thought about her actions that day in the bank. She explained, "You know, the morning I was in the bank, my husband and I had lost our store, our home, our car—everything we had. We have since moved to a small town near Austin. We're trying to pick up the pieces and start over again." She didn't have to say she was sorry. She had come to vindicate herself in her own way. I'm glad I was not rude to her. Although I've never lost a home or car, I've lived long enough to never say never.

When dealing in customer service, we do not know what people are experiencing in their lives. Our responsibility is not how people treat us, but how we respond to them.

Mrs. Thompson
(short version)

As we are interacting with customers, we need to understand that there are circumstances that dictate how people behave. When I was the customer service manager at NorthPark Bank, there was a lady who came in quite irate. She used a lot of vulgarity and talked about me in front of everyone. When she finished, a man came up and asked me how I could stand there and take that. I said to him, "I'm doing everything I can for her. I'm none of those names she called me. I know who I am." Six years later, the lady attended one of my seminars. She came up to me and asked, "Do you remember me?" I said, "Yes." She then told me that the day she was in the bank she and her husband had lost everything they had. I was glad I had not been rude to her. You never know what people are going through. It's our responsibility to respond to our customers with sensitivity and understanding.

The stories above illustrate the importance of timing your stories. Make sure they give enough pertinent information for the story to be meaningful. I suggest: never memorize a story or speech to the point that you can't adjust––in a moment's notice––without losing your composure.

QUESTION 4

Will The Listeners Appreciate This Story?

Many speakers try to set the tone for their speech and relax the listener with a funny story. That's fine, but realize that people sometimes laugh at things they find offensive. They sometimes laugh because they are embarrassed with the content of the story.

Vulgarity, profanity, ethnic and religious slurs, too much sex, overselling yourself, "put downs", criticisms, too much politics, mocking dialects, insider stories between you and a few audience members, too much blood and guts—aren't appreciated or appropriate for most audiences.

For example, a professional speaker was invited to a small, rural town to give a speech. When he got up to speak, he started making jokes about the dialect of small town folks. He talked about how backwards they were and how simple their lives were. To say the least, they were offended. Many people got up and left; others talked about running him out of town.

Of course, this is an extreme situation because most of us would use better judgment. But, have you ever been in the audience when a speaker failed to use good judgment? A good rule to remember is to use tact. It is best to avoid subjects that may offend.

Many speakers like to use human interest stories, but even a human interest story can be inappropriate in some situations. Be careful: when in doubt, throw it out.

She Got Involved

A woman was sitting with her children in a movie theater when she noticed that the boy sitting next to her wouldn't keep still. Annoyed, she glanced sideways and gasped. The boy's companion, a man in his 60's, was fondling him. The lady asked the manager to call the police, but he wouldn't. When the movie ended, she grabbed her children's hands and began trailing the man and the boy into a nearby shop. The lady approached the store manager and asked him to call the police. At first, he refused to get involved too. But after she pleaded, he finally let her use the phone to call the police. Officers arrived soon after the man and boy had left. The woman told the police what she had seen, and when she arrived home, a police message was on her answering machine: "Thanks. You've saved the life of a little boy. The man has been arrested."

This story originally reported by Mary Ellen Strote for **Moxie** is an example of a good human interest story that could illustrate a point about courage or the difference our actions can make in the lives of others, but is it appropriate? Molestation is a delicate subject. Audience members might feel uncomfortable and forget the main point. Therefore, be in tune to the pulse of your audience and tailor your stories accordingly.

Subjects like death, disease, abortion, abuse, racism, and religious beliefs, if not carefully constructed and delivered, can be offensive to some listeners. Best advice: if you are apprehensive that a story could be offensive, don't use it. There are many stories that can dramatize your point and make it clear.

QUESTION 5

Can I Illustrate The Point In An Effective Way Without Telling A Story?

Stories are a great way to empower people, but you may decide that another method best illustrates your particular point. There are several ways to add emphasis to your message.

Action Steps.   Step 1. Believe in yourself.
                     Step 2. Be assertive.
Steps can give the listener something to do immediately to accomplish a desired result. **Action steps are important when guiding the listener through a process.**

Factual information. According to the U. S. Bureau of Labor Statistics, the Five Fastest Growing Occupations by 1995 are: computer service technicians, legal assistants, computer systems analysts, computer programmers and computer operators. **Facts add credibility to your speech.**

Quotation. Henry Ford once said, "If you think you can, or you think you cannot, you're always right." **Quotes from familiar people are impressive.**

Statistics. According to a survey by medical researchers, the situations that cause you the most anxiety are: 74% of people experience anxiety when partying with strangers; 70% feel anxiety when giving a speech; and 65% are anxious when asked personal questions in public. **Statistics can arouse the analytical thinkers.**

Survey. A survey of 120 medium-size and large corporations by Accountemps, a temporary service agency, showed that the average worker spent 34% of his or her day "goofing off." That added up to about four months of extra paid vacation a year. **Surveys help shape people's opinions.**

Acronyms. Thelma Wells' motto is, "You can be the best of what you want to 'bee'." It means: B — Be aware of who you are; E — Eliminate the negatives from your life; E — Expect the best from people. **People will remember meaningful acronyms.**

Games. 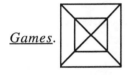 How many triangles do you see?

There are 16 triangles in this drawing. **Experience proves that brainteasers and games generate participation and discussion.**

Example. "People believe what you tell them if you say it enough; for example. . . ." Many times examples are stories, but they can also be metaphors or analogies. **Examples add clarity to your statements.**

Analogy. Public speaking is much like sculpting. You decide what image you want to create, choose your tools, study your materials and begin to mold. **Analogies show parallels that help make ideas clear.**

Question. Have you ever wondered why life's not fair? **Questions challenge, add curiosity and get attention.**

Testimony. More Americans are exercising than ever before, reports American Health Magazine. **Testimonies convey authority.**

Metaphor.   If we speak with conviction, we just might bear a fruit so sweet it feeds the hungry. **Metaphors add vibrance to your speech.**

Paraphrase. "Mr. X, you said . . . Is that right?" **Paraphrasing enables you to clearly understand questions, answers and comments from listeners.**

Humor. My doctor suggested I try running in place. I asked, "In place of what?" **Humor relaxes.**

Visual Aids. Visual aids enable listeners to visualize your point. **Slides, overheads, video presentations, flip charts, props and music engage the senses.**

Role play. Let's pretend you're running XYZ company. What would you do if . . . ? **Role playing helps to create empathy.**

A good speech employs all of these methods or a mix of them. Whatever you decide, you should capture the audience's attention and guide them in the direction they need to go.

In conclusion, when you are deciding whether or not you should tell a story, ask yourself:

1. What point do I want to make?
2. Do I know how to tell the story to make it powerful?
3. Do I have adequate time for a story?
4. Will the listeners appreciate the story?
5. Can I illustrate the point in an effective way without telling a story?

When you are able to answer these questions, you will have completed the first milestone on the journey to capturing your audience through storytelling.

PART 2

Researching The Story

Stories can . . .
capture the imagination where logic fails.

QUESTION 1

Where Do I Find Material?

Stories are everywhere. Everyday experiences will give you stories to tell. You really do not have to look hard for moments of truth.

Moment of Truth

I was coming out of the Federal Building in downtown Dallas one morning when a lady walked up to me and asked me for a quarter. I immediately said, "I don't have a quarter!" She didn't look poor, but she didn't look professional either, so I turned her down. But as soon as I did, I felt guilty. "Miss, why do you need a quarter?" I asked after calling her back. She said, "I need to catch the bus and I've lost my purse." I reached in my pocket and proved to her that I had lied. I gave her all the change in my pocket. But as I crossed the street to get into my air conditioned car, I examined my motives. I said, "Thelma Wells, you should be a shamed of yourself. You judged that lady solely by the way she looked."

I tell this story in my cultural diversity seminar to stress the need to eradicate negative stereotypes. In the story, I try to show how easily we subconsciously judge others by their race, clothes, speech, tone of voice, etc. When this experience happened to me many years ago, I didn't foresee that this story would enable listeners in my cultural diversity seminar to better understand the subtle prejudices we all share.

Always be on the look out for material. A personal experience may be a perfect anecdote years later.

31

Use stories from the media. When using stories from newspapers, magazines, commercials, movies and television programs, acknowledge the source and be correct in citing it. Don't recite a borrowed story unless you credit the source. If someone in the audience knows it's not your personal story, it could be humiliating. Believe me, there will be someone in the audience who will remember where he or she heard the story before. It's just not worth your reputation. Integrity is everything in any profession.

When you use stories from documents, I suggest having a copy of the document to show to the audience. Give them the date, name of the paper, and the author. For example, in **The Storytelling Magazine**, Winter 1992, there is an article entitled "Telling Tales About Science and Math" by Jenny Nash. It really struck me because many years ago I was a typing teacher. I taught football players how to type—or at least I tried. I'm glad to know that now storytelling is becoming a part of the curriculum of many schools. This article [show it] says, "Too many kids think math and science are dull, difficult or scary." Stories can help change those perceptions by factoring in creativity and adventure.

Notice I mentioned who, what, when, where and why in describing the article and its use. I mixed a short story with the factual information and proved its authenticity by showing the article. Whether you use personal stories or find stories in documented material, it is up to you. I suggest you do both. But, don't be afraid to look at your life first for your unique stories. These signature stories will set you apart from everyone else.

Use real life situations. Look at your past and present. Examine your life and the lessons you have learned. What are your triumphs? What mistakes have made you a better person? A good personal story will relate to the listeners and challenge them to learn something new about their lives. Look for stories from your culture, your circle of friends, your family and your hobbies. Many private moments of truth can be powerful tools for growth.

You can find stories in:

* Your childhood
* Your school days
* Your athletic participation
* Your talents and skills
* Your mistakes
* Your most embarrassing moments
* Your college life
* Your first boyfriend or girlfriend
* Your first trip away from home
* Your hobbies
* Your projects
* Your expectations
* Your shortcomings
* Your heroic deeds
* Your spouse
* Your children
* Your pet
* Your spiritual experiences
* Your causes
* Your values
* Your travels
* Your work

Perhaps this small list will provoke some thought for your stories. The best stories are ones that are dear to you. If you are willing to visualize your life as a compilation of interesting stories, it shouldn't be too difficult to find some interesting ones to tell.

QUESTION 2

Can I Use Other People's Stories?

One summer I was in the audience when a speaker was addressing an association. The young lady started telling a story and everyone began murmuring and whispering. There was such a commotion that I touched the man next to me and asked, "What's going on?" He whispered, "The speaker yesterday told that same story as if it was his story." In fact, it could have been either speakers' personal story. But when both told the same story, they both lost credibility.

People associate stories with the teller.

I am flattered by those who have asked me for permission to use my stories. When I agree with the context in which they will be used, I feel more comfortable in granting permission. However, even if written permission is granted, when a story is recited by too many speakers, as in the incident above, the reputation of each speaker is at stake. Everyone who hears it more than once will wonder, "Whose story is it?" If, however, the story's origin is well known, everyone might say, "He's trying to be like ____," or, "She's starting to sound like ___."

One winter I attended a convention, and one of the speakers used several stories from the book of a famous trainer, practically word for word. Again, this caused a bit of an uproar among the audience. If the speaker had worked for the trainer and the stories were a part of the curriculum, it might have been appropriate for the speaker to use the stories. However, the same rule of appropriate credit would apply. The trainer would still receive credit for his or her stories. In this instance, because the speaker failed to give appropriate credit, his image was scarred. Personal style and image are essential.

35

The National Speakers Association has outlined ethical guidelines for its members to follow when using the stories or works of others. To get a copy of these guidelines, contact:

> National Speakers Association
> 1500 S. Priest Drive
> Tempe, Arizona 85281
> (602) 968-2552
> Fax: (602) 968-0911

According to The World Book Dictionary, Plagiarism is, "An idea, expression, plot, etc. taken from another and used as one's own. In the words of William Hazlett, "If an author is once detected in borrowing, he will be suspected of plagiarism ever after."

Bottom line—plagiarism, like stealing, is a crime. Whenever you use signature works from other speakers, you are required to get written permission; and you should use the material only as you pledge to use it.

The story is told of a trainer who gave a speaker written permission to use some of her material in a seminar. Face-to-face, they discussed the material and the trainer signed each page of the material giving her consent. Several months later, the speaker was accused by the trainer of using unauthorized material. However, the speaker could prove the authorization.

Some speakers have been financially, emotionally and professionally ruined by law suits resulting from alleged plagiarism. Don't be caught in this tangled web. Many speakers say the same thing, but say it differently, each adding their own ingenuity and personality. Best advice: "Do the right thing."

The document on the following page may be useful when you are seeking permission to use another's material.

SAMPLE PERMISSION FORM*

I am preparing a speech entitled *Capture Your Audience Through Storytelling* to address corporate managers at XYZ company. I request permission to include stories/passages from your speech [book, handout, newsletter, etc.] as outlined below.

(Insert Outline)

I would like permission to include the excerpts any time I speak on Storytelling throughout the world. I understand in order to use your copyrighted work in written material, I would need to obtain further written permission.

Please indicate on this form the acknowledgement you would like to be given as the owner of the work.

PERMISSION GRANTED BY: _____
DATE: _____

ACKNOWLEDGEMENT TO READ: _____
_____

Thank you for your prompt attention.

_____

Most of the time signed permission is not necessary. If you verbally credit your source, that's usually sufficient. However, if you are planning to use several works from a source or you are unsure whether the source would approve of you using his or her signature material, get written permission. You will rest easier and feel more confident when presenting the information in your speech.

*This is a sample only. It does not represent a legal document. Please consult a licensed attorney for professional legal advice.

QUESTION 3

What Subjects Create The Best Impact?

Childhood experiences, human interest, sports, society, nature, pets, children, spouse, sad stories with happy endings, personal tragedy with a point and a purpose--can impact the listener in a powerful way. But truly, just about every experience is a subject that can create impact if you:

- Build a sense of suspense or joy
- Give details to enable the listener to visualize the scene
- Build rapport so that the listener identifies with the story
- Engage the listener emotionally
- Challenge the listener to change, learn and/or act
- Focus the listener on a particular goal or point

Courageous Stranger

Barbara Ramsey was driving down U.S. Route 1 near Ashland, Va., when she was rear-ended by another vehicle, and her car caught fire. Desperately, she pulled her two year old son, Zachary, from his seat and tried to get out of the car. Unable to open the door or the windows, she tried breaking the glass with her feet. It wouldn't break. Barbara and Zachary were trapped.

A stranger and his wife were driving toward Barbara when the collision occurred. They saw an orange ball of fire that nearly covered four lanes and pulled over. The stranger ran to see what he could do. But ten feet from the car, the flames stopped him short. He felt helpless, but more than that, he feared he might already be too late.

Suddenly he saw two feet in white socks push on the car window. He knew he had to do something fast. Inside the car, Barbara had given up hope. Flames had already burned both her and Zachary. She picked up Zachary and told him they were going to die.

38

The stranger found a dead tree about 14 feet long. He thrust it through an opening in the window, but the tree broke. He then swung the broken trunk like a baseball bat and the glass shattered. Barbara handed Zachary to the stranger and then jumped out. Both she and her son suffered third degree burns, but their lives were saved.

This simple human interest story out of the **Herald-Progress** reported by Sarah McLeod creates impact. It's packed with suspense. The details enable the listener to vividly visualize the scene. Most anyone can identify with the stranger's dilemma in risking his life. It's emotionally engaging. It challenges the listener to pay attention and anticipate a conclusion, and it focuses the listener on the nobility of courage.

Impact is created from suspense when the listeners can "see" the scene in their minds, identify with the characters and get involved in the story.

QUESTION 4

Can I Overdo Storytelling?

Yes! You can overdo storytelling. You can tell so many stories that the listener forgets what you are trying to say. If your story is too long, has no climax, or if the listeners have heard it too many times, it's overdone.

QUESTION 5

How Much Time Should I Devote To A Single Story?

You should devote as much time as is absolutely necessary to make the story work, but remember that certain extenuating circumstances could interrupt your story, so keep it simple. A good story is simple, straightforward and clear.

QUESTION 6

Can My Stories Diminish My Credibility Or My Topic?

Your stories may diminish your credibility when you leave out pertinent information, sound unprepared, indulge in too much fantasy, cite confusing details, or use vulgar or profane language.

QUESTION 7

How Can I Document The Authenticity Of My Personal Stories?

Use dates, times, places and names—who, what, when, where, why and how. You should also show-and-tell materials such as slides, photographs, documents and maps when available.

QUESTION 8

When Is The Best Time During My Presentation To Tell A Story?

The best time to tell a story during your presentation is when you are sure it is appropriate and will accomplish your goal. It does not matter whether it is in the introduction, middle or end. (Refer to Part 1, Question 1, for a review of "Make A Point—Tell A Story.")

PART 3

Telling The Story

Stories can . . .
get attention when thoughts wander,
and pack a powerful punch.

QUESTION 1

Am I Involving The Listeners As A Part Of The Story?

Life Is Tough

One day while driving south on Central Expressway in Dallas, I noticed a bumper sticker that read, "Life is tough and then you die!" That was not what I needed that day. The motivator needed motivating. I was already having a pity party and this bumper sticker seemed to confirm my thoughts; so I reread it. It said, "Life is tough and then you die!" I thought, "You know, that's the truth. Life is hard and then you die."

That same day, I turned and went north on Central and rode past a car dealer's billboard. The flashing lights on the kiosk said, "Tough times never last, but tough people do!" I said, "Oh, what a relief." I wondered where I had heard that before and remembered Dr. Robert Schuller from the Crystal Cathedral in Garden Grove, Calif. That's one of his mottos. He says, "Tough times never last, but tough people do!" I thought, "Thank you, Dr. Schuller. I really needed that. Life is worth living."

When involving the listeners as a part of the story, ask yourself:

- Can they identify with the situation?
- Can they visualize the situation?
- Will they want resolution?

46

Most people can identify with being "down in the dumps." It's a part of living. Most people can visualize riding in a car reading bumper stickers because it's a common experience. And most people will want a positive resolution instead of one that leaves the listener up in the air or depressed.

Listeners should be able to identify and visualize your story as you speak. If they can't, they will give you cues. Notice the listeners' facial expression and body language. Are their faces blank? Are their eyes glazed over? Are they leaning forward in anticipation and agreement or are they slouching over? If you notice too many eyes closed or shifting, rather than assuming your listeners are sleeping or day dreaming, perhaps changing your tone is needed. Change your inflection, use appropriate "pregnant pauses", maintain eye contact and use body language. If these suggestions don't have the desired impact, consider changing the content or the length. Involving the listener as a part of the story isn't difficult, but it does take practice.

QUESTION 2

Am I Creating A Climax
With Resolution?

The climax is simply the lesson—the high point of the story which leads toward a resolution. It must be relevant and realistic.

"I Need A Credit Card"

It was 11:30 P.M. on an October evening when I entered an airport in Washington, D.C. I rushed to a car rental station fearful that the representatives might be gone and concerned about my long drive that night to Indianhead, Md. I raced to the rental station and presented my driver's license and confirmation number to the agent. I politely asked her to put my driver's license and confirmation numbers into the computer to activate my rental profile. She replied quite firmly, "I need a credit card!" I said, "I understand your procedure, but if you put my driver's license and confirmation numbers into the computer, you will find my profile with instructions about the rental car." She more profoundly stated, "I said, I need a credit card before I can get you a car."

Attempting to remain calm, I said again, "I understand, but trust me. I've done this many times before all over the United States. I just left a car in Houston. Please do as I ask." Arrogantly, she replied, "I don't care what you did in Houston; you are now in Washington, D.C., and I said I need a credit card!"

Well—that did it! I shouted, "Woman, you had better put this information into the computer because I WILL get a rental car. I AM driving to Indianhead, Md., even if I have to take you with me. Do you understand?"

A gentleman co-worker overheard the shouting and asked to help. He put the information into the computer and presto— the profile came up. Nevertheless, I couldn't stop arguing.

48

I continued, "You don't know who I am. I teach customer service to people all over the world. I teach people how to stay calm when they encounter rude people like you. I'm tired [and on and on]." Twenty-five minutes later, I finally started on my drive to Indianhead.

Did the representative make me angry? Well, you might be surprised by my answer, but 'no'. I became upset because of the extenuating circumstances. It was late and I was tired. I still had a long drive ahead of me, and I had been informed earlier that day that the inn where I was staying locked its doors at midnight. Frankly, I was scared.

Similar situations had happened to me on other occasions. However, I remained calm and in control. Fortunately, it was earlier in the day and I had time to spare. The fact of the matter is nobody should have the power to make you angry. We respond to people based on emotions like fear. Incidentally, when I finally arrived at the Indianhead Inn, the front desk agent had left a note for me on the door, "I waited until midnight. I left." What a night!

I tell this story hoping to create a resolution that can be used to help others learn to cope with anger. When creating your climax, ask yourself:

- Does the climax achieve my goals for the listener?

- Does the climax carry the listener to new directions or a surprise ending?

- Will the climax challenge, arouse and/or impact the listener the way I desire?

- Will the resolution enable the listener to learn new concepts, gain insights or develop a new attitude?

QUESTION 3

Does The Climax Achieve My Goals For The Listener?

An extremely good example of goal setting in storytelling is this story by David Armstrong, COO of Armstrong International and author of *Managing by Storying Around: A New Method of Leadership*, published by Doubleday/Currency, 1992.

Sweetened Iced Tea

It was a hot day in July. A salesperson and I had just finished making a sales call, and while driving to our next appointment, we decided to stop and get a cold drink. We pulled into a truck-stop restaurant. I ordered an iced tea.

"Could you bring me some Sweet 'n Low with that, please?" I asked.

"The sugar is on the table," the waitress replied.

"Yes, but it doesn't dissolve in iced tea as well as Sweet 'n Low does," I told her.

"I'm sorry, that's all we have."

When the waitress came back with our drinks, she placed a small metal cup down next to my iced tea.

"I'm sorry we don't have any Sweet 'n Low", she said.

"But I took hot water and poured it over some sugar to help dissolve it. I hope that's okay."

Now that's service!

On the way out, I went up to the waitress and gave her a $2 tip for my 60-cent iced tea, and I thanked her for the best service I'd had in a long time. You should have seen her co-workers' expressions. There is no such thing as a commodity. Everything —even a glass of iced tea—can be differentiated on service.

50

Armstrong teaches skills to his employees by simply telling them stories. It's a great way to manage. With each story, he has specific goals. For the "Sweetened Iced Tea" story, he writes:

The Moral of The Story:

* *Good service will generate future business.* Will I eat at the truck stop the next time I'm in the area? You bet. Will I tell everyone I know about the service I received? I already have. I've told this story 50 times.

* *Good service should exist everywhere.* Remember, I got this service at a truck stop, not a five-star restaurant. At Armstrong, good service should be found in every department, not just sales.

* *Good service should be rewarded.* If we see a colleague providing good service, we should praise her. If we receive good service, we should do everything possible to encourage it. I made a point of making a big deal out of the service I received, in front of the waitress's co-workers. I gave her a 333 percent tip.

When we are training, delivering a keynote or facilitating a meeting, our stories, like Armstrong's, should achieve specific goals for the listener.

QUESTION 4

Does The Climax Carry The Listener To New Directions Or A Surprise Ending?

Listeners must be able to relate to the ending of the story. In "I Need a Credit Card," I brought the conclusion to a surprise ending and left a little suspense over what finally happened to me that night. Did I find another inn? Did I sleep in my car? The purpose for this suspenseful twist is to keep the listener alert. It is also a great lead into another story. (By the way, I did find an inn about 40 miles away.)

QUESTION 5

Will The Climax Challenge, Arouse And/Or Impact The Listener The Way I Desire?

Catch Me If You Can

I ran away from a broken home at age 16. I successfully impersonated a Pan American airline pilot for two years. At 18, I became the chief resident of a Georgia hospital posing as a pediatrician. I practiced medicine there for about a year. At age 19, having never been to law school, I took and passed the bar exam in the state of Louisiana under an assumed name and, before my 19th birthday was over, I became the Assistant General Attorney. I left Louisiana after a year and moved to Provo, Utah

52

where I posed as a Ph.D. in sociology. By my 21st birthday, I had been a millionaire twice—having cashed over $2.5 million dollars in bad checks. Some people have wondered how a 16 year old was able to get away with this? Journalists have said that it was my upbringing, my mannerisms, my appearance.

I ran away from home at age 16 eventhough I had been blessed with parents who taught me right from wrong. But, after 22 years of marriage, my parents chose to get a divorce, and I was asked to choose with which parent I wanted to live. I couldn't make that choice. I never did. Instead I ran away from home and saw my mother many years later, but I never saw my father again.

I was 6 feet tall at age 16. I always had a little gray hair. It was easy for me to pose 10 years older than my actual age. As an impostor and thief, I forged checks in over 26 countries. I was the youngest person ever to be put on the FBI's 10 most wanted list. I was caught—only once—at age 21 in France. Twenty-one countries filed suits against me for forgery. I served time in other countries and in the United States until a group of U.S. Senators felt they could use my knowledge to help develop procedures to prevent fraud inside governmental agencies.

I was given a second chance by the American government, and also by a young girl who fell in love with me and turned my life around. Today, our three children have shaped my perception of life. Life is not difficult to understand as I had once thought—its all about family. I've learned that success isn't measured by money, but by love in ones family. My life, though many think it was exciting, was not complete without my family.

Many people throughout the world know the remarkable story of Frank Abagnale. This paraphased version of Abagnale's true story, taken from his audiocassette tape and book *Catch Me If You Can*, impacts the listener in an astounding manner. First, the listener is spellbound by the astounding facts of his early life. Then Abagnale challenges and emotionally moves the listener to the climax—a lesson about the love of family. Abagnale's story is unique, but you too can use facts and emotion to challenge, arouse and/or impact your listeners the way you desire.

53

QUESTION 6

Will The Resolution Enable The Listener To Learn New Concepts, Gain Insights Or Develop A New Attitude?

Each story told in this section enabled the listener to either learn a new concept, gain insights or develop a new attitude from the resolution. "I Need A Credit Card" taught the listener that anger is an emotion controlled by extenuating circumstances. "Sweetened Iced Tea" enabled the employees at Armstrong International to gain insights into the benefits of good service. "Catch Me If You Can" helped to form a new attitude in some listeners about the importance of the love of ones family.

When you are telling your story, it is imperative to:
* Involve the listener as a part of the story, and
* Create a climax with resolution.

When you do these things, you will have listeners sitting on the edge of their chairs and hanging on every word.

QUESTION 7

Am I An Effective Storyteller?

The greater percentage of communication is received through nonverbal channels.

7% words
38% tone of voice
55% body language

— "Communication Without Words," **Personnel Journal**, January 1989.

If a story isn't told well, it doesn't matter how vital the information. Our effectiveness as storytellers depends on our vocabulary, our tone of voice and our body language.

Here are a few tips to enable you to effectively deliver a story.

Be a writer. You don't have to be a good writer to be a good speaker and vice versa. But, when you get your stories down on paper, you'll notice that your stories will become more detailed, more fluent and more clear. You have the power in words to heal or hurt, educate or confuse, encourage or deflate, humble or humiliate, condone or condemn, unify or separate. Choose your words carefully because with each string of sentences, you should impart knowledge and wisdom.

Be an artist. Just as an artist uses a canvas and strokes of a brush to create paintings, words eloquently spoken through stories can paint indelible pictures in the minds of the listeners. For example, come with me on vacation. Let's retreat to Montego Bay, Jamaica. It's 8:30 P.M. We're on the beach reclining in blue beach chairs surrounded by white sand. Beside our blue chairs are small, round glass topped tables holding a tall frosty glass of iced tea. Inside the glass are fresh, green mint leaves, a red, plump, round cherry and a slice of navel orange. We're resting and feeling the breeze against our bodies. Magnificent colors reflect off the water. The billowing waves splash gently upon the shore. Our souls are refreshed. Our vacation is complete. Like the stroke of a brush, the sound of words can create a picture in the mind of the listener that could last forever.

Be an actor. Dramatize your stories, but don't over dramatize them. I believe that dramatizing means having the ability to act out your story in such a way that the audience believes what you are saying. You want to be believable. Add appropriate gestures, facial expressions and body movements. If your mouth is saying one thing and your gestures another, your story may be misinterpreted. Visualize in your mind your story and act it out while you're speaking. Also, visualize the response you want to receive from the audience.

Be an orator. Voice inflection, pronunciation, enunciation, volume, speed, pauses, accents, silence—make or break your story. Develop your 'gift of speech' by learning more about the correct usage of these and other techniques that will help you grow in your presentation skills.

Be yourself. Being a writer, actor, artist and orator is "much ado about nothing" if you, the speaker, are not genuine. People will eventually see straight through your fluff. Remember: words uttered from the heart will be felt in the hearts of others.

From The Heart
(Thelma's Story)

It's 8:36 A.M. on May 30, 1993. I am driving on Highway 183 in Dallas coming from the airport. I have a knot in my stomach the size of a canteloupe. I'm thinking about the upcoming National Speakers Association Annual Convention and about the awesome responsibility I have to people who pay me to speak to them. I consider my duty as a speaker to impart a message that can change a life, enhance a company's bottom-line, encourage employees to higher productivity, challenge people to higher goals and dreams and I reflect on how all this came to be.

I was born in 1941 to my mother who, during birth, suffered a stroke and became paralyzed. Unable to care for me, she allowed my great grandmother, Granny Sarah Harrell, to take and raise me.

We were poor though I didn't know it. I always wore the finest clothes, hand-me-downs, from Granny's employers. Granny was always on the go. She could do everything—wash, iron, cook, sew, clean, work in someone's kitchen, clean up their house and then go to church. She would always say, "An idle mind is the devil's workshop."

Following in her footsteps, I became actively involved in church and community affairs. She taught me how to keep a smile on my face even when I'm down. She'd say, "God will take care of you." And I believed her.

Growing up, I really didn't know what I wanted to be, but I knew I wanted more than the circumstances and the system provided at that time for African Americans. In 1959, I enrolled at North Texas State University just as it was integrating. It wasn't easy. At first, I couldn't live on campus because there were a token few rooms allocated for minority students. These were already filled; therefore, I was forced to seek housing "across the tracks." After the daily, lengthy walk to the college campus, I encountered

58

certain professors who refused to acknowledge my presence in class even though I was properly enrolled. Nonetheless, I graduated in 1963 to become a substitute teacher.

I have high esteem for those in the teaching profession because they are directly involved in educating others. At the time I was teaching, I was trying to help football players learn to type. Unfortunately, training them how to behave towards a young, female instructor took the entire class period. But, I stuck with it until I heard that John Deere Company in Dallas was looking for a secretary. I applied and was hired.

You have to be careful for what you pray. Four years later I wanted a change and asked God to give it to me. My prayers were answered. I got pregnant and sick with my third child and had to be laid off. Little did I know that I was on a path that led me to speaking. After my recovery, I decided I wanted to work for NorthPark National Bank. I don't remember why I was persistent in working for NorthPark National Bank, but I do remember asking, begging and pleading for a job until the human resource manager finally broke down and gave me an entry level position. I started in the new accounts department and over several years worked myself up to Assistant Vice President over Customer Service and other areas.

I had learned a lot about myself and about people by then. My life had been a series of stories that reinforced that I could be the best if I believed. In 1976, I started teaching banking courses. I noticed the fear my students experienced just before exams, so I started teaching them self-esteem techniques. Their grades shot up. They appreciated the motivation and a few requests for me to speak began to trickle in. I realized then I could make a career of speaking if I tried. This was over 13 years ago. Back then professional speaking wasn't a hot career. Only the big names and athletes really made money, but it was worth a try. At first, I kept my job at the bank—which was smart. I waited until both my husband and I agreed I should pursue speaking full time. In 1984, I took a chance.

Who would have ever thought that a black girl from the projects would be traveling the globe touching people's lives with words and stories? On that highway in May 1993, as I looked over my life, as I thought of where my life stories had led me, I was challenged to teach from the lessons I live by.

I wear a bumblebee pin wherever I go. It is an outward symbol of my motto, "You can be the best of what you want to bee!" This saying was given to me one Sunday morning by a dear friend who noticed that I loved wearing bumblebee pins. She said, "Thelma Wells, whenever you wear that pin, remember the story of the bumblebee. It's not suppose to fly because its body is too big for its wings, but it does. Just like the bee, you can be the best of what you want to 'bee'."

Public speaking has given me the opportunity to 'bee' my best. I have had the pleasure of seeing my message change people's lives, help them make decisions, lift their spirits, give them hope and teach them skills.

Many of you reading this book are new speakers or have a burning desire to speak as a career. Let me encourage you, it's a wonderful, fulfilling and rewarding profession. Let me also warn you, professional speaking is hard work. Preparing a career in this business is much like any other. It takes 25 hours a day, 8 days a week, 32 days a month, and 366 days each year. There is reading and writing and researching and traveling and billing and collecting and scheduling and calling and networking and mailings and meetings and staffing and practicing and equipment and contracts and overhead and taxes and . . . SPEAKING. But it's worth it.

As you strive to bring out the best in others whether you are a speaker, executive, trainer, sales person, minister, teacher or parent, your stories should be a reflection of your life. When you speak the truth from your experiences and from your heart, your stories will live on in the memories of others. Tell the truth; and when you do, you'll be sure to capture your audience through storytelling.

Checklist

This checklist is a tool designed to remind you of questions to ask yourself when you are deciding to tell a story, researching a story or telling a story in your speech.

I. Deciding to Tell A Story: Use this checklist while planning your speech to decide the need for a story and its appropriateness for your audience.

☐ Should I tell a story?

☐ Why would I tell a story?

☐ What's the point I want to make?

☐ Is any other technique more effective?

☐ How much time do I have?

☐ Will listeners appreciate it?

☐ Is the story appropriate for its particular audience?

☐ Can I tell the story powerfully?

II. Researching The Story: Use this checklist after you have decided to tell a story as a resource to help you find the right story to tell to emphasize you point(s).

☐ Where can I find stories to tell?

☐ Should I use someone else's story?

☐ What kind of story would create the most impact for what I am trying to emphasize?

☐ Can I overdo storytelling?

61

☐ Have I timed the story?

☐ How does the story affect my credibility or topic?

☐ Am I creating the authenticity of the story with supporting facts? (Date, time, place, characters, etc.)

☐ Where in the presentation sequence does the story best fit?

III. Telling The Story: Use this checklist to analyze the effectiveness of your story, its lesson and your delivery.

☐ Am I involving the listener as a part of the story?

☐ Does the climax produce resolution?

☐ Does the climax achieve my goals for the listener?

☐ Does the climax carry the listener to a new direction or to a surprise ending?

☐ Will the climax challenge, arouse and/or impact the listener the way I desire?

☐ Will the resolution help the listener learn new concepts, gain insight or develop a new attitude?

☐ Am I an effective storyteller?

Suggestions for Opening Your Story

- Are you aware that . . .
- Believe it or not . . .
- Come with me . . .
- Follow me to . . .

- Have you heard the story about . . .
- Imagine . . .
- Just the other day . . .
- Listen to this story . . .
- How many of you have experienced . . .
- Have you ever been in a situation . . .
- Once upon a time . . .
- There's a story told about . . .
- Can you identify with . . .
- Visualize yourself . . .

Suggestions for Closing Your Story

- When we apply the lessons for the story we just heard . . .
- The essence of the story is . . .
- We learned from the story that . . .
- We can plainly see that . . .
- What would you have done if . . .
- What do you think happened in this story when . . .
- Like the person in the story, could you have . . .
- Let's think about this . . .
- In conclusion . . .

Recommended Reading

Storytelling Magazine, published quarterly, National Association for the Preservation and Perpetuation of Storytelling (NAPPS), P.O. Box 309, Jonesborough, Tenn. 37659.

Managing by Storying Around, David M. Armstrong, New York: Doubleday/Currency, 1992.

For Your Continuing Education

National Speakers Association, 1500 S. Priest Drive, Tempe, Arizona 85281, (602)986-2552.

Toastmasters (check you local telephone directory)

About the Author

Thelma Wells gives you the formula for effective speech making which has made her one of the nation's most successful motivators and corporate trainers. *Capture Your Audience Through Storytelling* grew out of a compilation of real life experiences that led to her rise as a successful business woman and speaker throughout the United States, United Kingdom, Asia, Australia and other parts of the world. She has taught the skills contained in this book to thousands of people at conventions hosted by the National Speakers Association. You'll discover the storytelling techniques that have packed her seminars—standing room only!

Thelma Wells has developed many programs and seminars for corporations, associations, religious and educational institutions—

Motivational Seminars: You Can Be The Best Of What You Want To Bee!; Self-Esteem Is A Matter of Choice; Building And Maintaining A Positive Mental Attitude.

Customer Service Programs: Exceptional Customer Service—A Must!; How To Use The Telephone As An Effective Customer Service Tool.

Corporate Diversity Program: Red and Yellow, Black and White--Valuing Cultural Diversity.

Other Seminars: Stress Or Distress—That's The Question?; Portraying A Professional Image.

Program information is available only from Thelma Wells & Associates. Please write or call:

Thelma Wells & Associates, 1402 Corinth, LB-124, Dallas, Texas 75215, Toll Free 800/843-5622, In Dallas 214/428-8635